The Wooden Horse of Troy

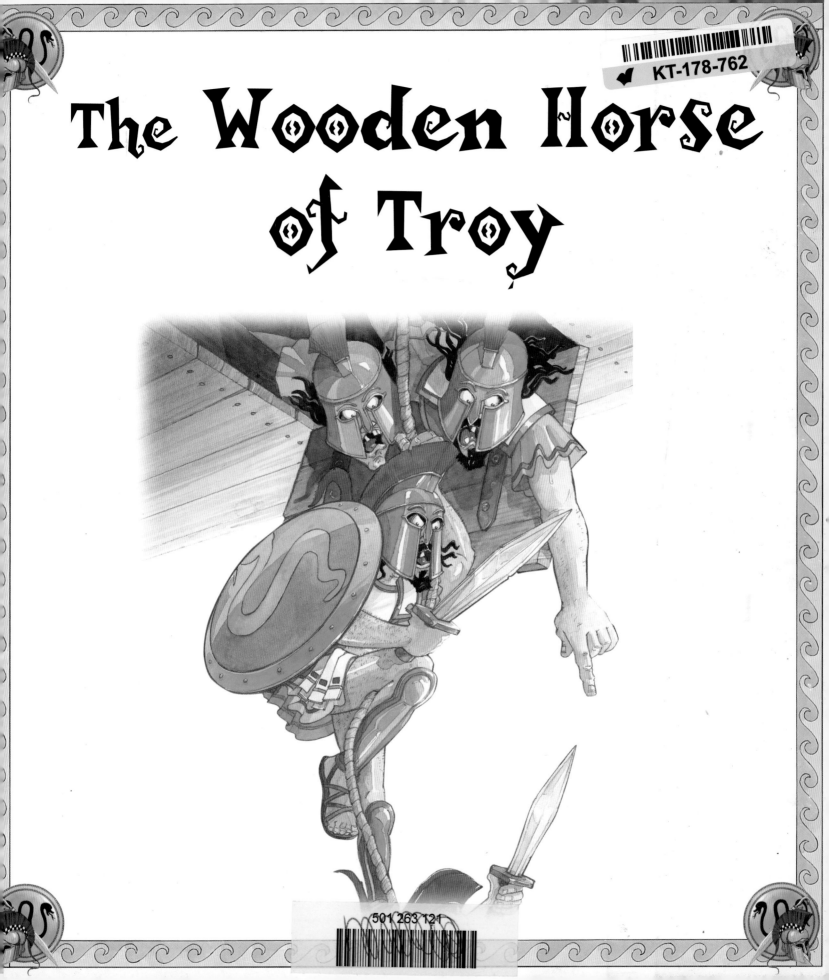

Author:
John Malam studied ancient history and
archaeology at the University of Birmingham, after
which he worked as an archaeologist at the Ironbridge
Gorge Museum, Shropshire. He is now a writer, editor
and reviewer, specialising in books for children.
His website is *www.johnmalam.co.uk*.

Artist:
Peter Rutherford was born in Ipswich. He studied
illustration and animation at Ipswich Art College and
then worked as an Art Director in several leading
London advertising agencies. He now lives and works
in Suffolk and has been illustrating children's books for
the past 10 years.

Series creator:
David Salariya was born in Dundee, Scotland.
He has illustrated a wide range of books and has
created and designed many new series for publishers
both in the UK and overseas. In 1989, he established
The Salariya Book Company. He lives in Brighton
with his wife, illustrator Shirley Willis, and their
son Jonathan.

Editor:
Michael Ford

Published in Great Britain in 2004 by
Book House, an imprint of
The Salariya Book Company Ltd
25 Marlborough Place, Brighton BN1 1UB

Please visit the Salariya Book Company at:
www.salariya.com
www.book-house.co.uk

ISBN 1 904642-30-6

A catalogue record for this book is available
from the British Library.

Printed and bound in China.

Printed on paper
from sustainable forests.

Ancient Greek Myths
The Wooden Horse of Troy

Written by
John Malam

Illustrated by
Peter Rutherford

Created and designed by
David Salariya

BOOK HOUSE

The world of Ancient Greek mythology

T he Ancient Greek civilisation was one of the greatest the world has witnessed. It reached its peak of success in the fifth century BC – nearly 2,500 years ago.

We owe much to the Ancient Greeks. They were great scientists, mathematicians, writers and thinkers. They were also brilliant storytellers. Many of the tales they told were in the form of poems, often thousands of lines long. The Greeks wrote poems on almost all kinds of human experience, such as love, friendship, war, revenge and history. The most famous of the poems which have passed down to us are epic tales of courage and warfare, where gods, heroes and monsters struggle against great odds.

A map showing the Ancient Greek mainland, surrounding islands and neighbouring lands

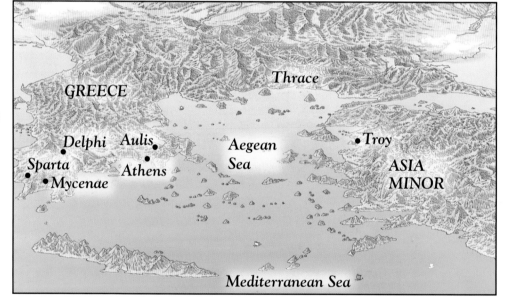

At first, all of their stories, lengthy as they were, were handed down from generation to generation by word of mouth. The people who told them were often travelling storytellers who performed in towns throughout the Greek world. They were called 'rhapsodes', which means 'song-stitchers'. As a rhapsode spoke or sang the words of his story, in a loud and clear voice, he stitched its many twists and turns together to make a beginning, a middle and an end. In time, the stories were written down. What follows is one version of the Wooden Horse of Troy. It is a tale about the Trojan War, when a Greek army laid siege to the city of Troy, and how, by trickery, they defeated the Trojans.

If you need help with any of the names, go to the pronunciation guide on page 31.

introduction

Greetings citizens! Gather round! I am the rhapsode – the teller of stories. You may have heard of the great siege at Troy – the beautiful woman who caused the conflict, the brave warriors who fought and fell for what they believed and the trickery that finally ended it all. Lend me your ears for...

I come this day from far away
With a tale to tell that spins a spell,
Which you will hear – if you draw near –
Of times of old and heroes bold.

So gather round and hear my story
Which I will weave from ancient glory,
By joining threads from start to end –
Then you may pass it to a friend.

Now, let me check the sources...

5

Troy – built with the gods' help

My story begins long, long ago, in an age when immortal gods mixed with humans on Earth. The great Zeus sent his son, Apollo, and his brother, Poseidon, to work among men. It was a punishment, because they had rebelled against him. For one whole year Apollo and Poseidon worked for Laomedon, the King of Troy, building strong walls around his city. But they had not worked alone. They asked Aeacus, one of the humans, to help.

Laomedon had promised his famous immortal horses as payment for the gods' help. But he broke his promise when the work was completed. Apollo sent a plague upon Troy and Poseidon ordered a monstrous sea serpent to attack the city. Laomedon visited an oracle to seek advice and was told he must sacrifice his daughter, Hesione, to the serpent. But he could not bear to lose her. Instead, he promised his horses to whoever killed the monster. This brave deed fell to the hero Heracles but, again, Laomedon broke his promise.

The snakes that foretold the future

When the walls of Troy were built, three snakes slithered to the top of them. The two snakes that climbed the parts built by the gods fell down dead. However, the snake that climbed the wall built by Aeacus slid into the city. Apollo said it was a sign that Troy would be taken over by the descendants of Aeacus.

What did Heracles do?

Heracles was angry because Laomedon had not given up his horses. He left Troy, but returned many years later to kill Laomedon and his sons. Hesione successfully pleaded with Heracles to spare her brother, Podarces, who from then on was known as Priam – the new King of Troy.

The judgement of Paris

In time, King Priam and his wife, Hecabe, had a son called Paris. However, before the child's birth, Hecabe had a nightmare that she would give birth to a flaming torch. She thought this was a bad omen and was afraid of her new son, so she left baby Paris to die on a mountain. But he didn't. Luckily, he was found by a shepherd who raised him as his own son.

Paris grew into a fine young man who worked as a shepherd. One day, as he tended his flock, he came upon three goddesses: Hera, Athena and Aphrodite. They were arguing over a golden apple, upon which was written "For the most beautiful". They asked Zeus to decide, but he ordered Paris to be the judge. Hera offered to give him Asia and Europe if he chose her; Athena vowed to make him a great warrior; Aphrodite promised him Helen, the most beautiful woman in the world. Overcome with love for Helen, Paris gave the apple to Aphrodite.

The Apple of Strife

A goddess called Eris had thrown the apple amongst the goddesses, because they had been invited to a wedding and she had not. She knew they would argue over who was the most beautiful of them all.

8

Ask the storyteller

Did Paris choose wisely?

Poor Paris. He allowed himself to be tempted by the bribes of the goddesses and let his heart rule his head. His love for Helen was strong, but in choosing her his fate was sealed, as was that of the city of Troy.

I choose your gift, goddess Aphrodite.

Paris takes Helen to Troy

Many men had asked for Helen's hand in marriage. But her father Tyndareus, King of Sparta, would only let her marry on one condition – that all the men who loved her would always protect her. They agreed and swore an oath. Helen was free to choose a husband and she picked a noble called Menelaus, from the city of Mycenae.

Ten years had passed since Paris's meeting with the three goddesses. During this time Paris had returned to Troy and was accepted back into his real family. But Aphrodite had not forgotten her promise to him. She waited until Menelaus was away from Sparta, then took Paris to meet Helen. With a little help from Aphrodite, Paris led Helen to his ship at night, loaded it with treasure, then sailed away back to Troy.

When Menelaus discovered what had happened, he was furious.

A last resort

At first, Menelaus tried to get Helen back by peaceful means. He went to Troy and pleaded for his wife's safe return, but all his demands were rejected. From then on, he knew that the only way to win Helen's freedom was by defeating the Trojans in war.

Ask the storyteller

Why did Helen go with Paris?

Aphrodite cast a powerful spell over Helen, making her fall in love with Paris. Some say the goddess made Paris look like Menelaus, tricking Helen into believing she was with her husband.

The fleet sails to Troy

Menelaus visited his brother, Agamemnon, King of Mycenae, to ask for help. Agamemnon called on all the men who had sworn to protect Helen. In this way the Greeks assembled an army, with Agamemnon as their leader.

Agamemnon gathered one thousand ships at the port of Aulis, ready to take the Greek army across the sea to Troy. But a prophet, Calchas, said the fleet must not sail until Achilles had joined them, because Troy could only be conquered with the hero's help. Calchas, who was skilled in reading signs sent by the gods, saw a snake which ate nine sparrows and then turned itself into stone. He said this omen meant that Troy would only be captured after ten years of war. Calchas's next prophecy was grim: Agamemnon must sacrifice his own daughter, Iphigeneia, to please the gods. So, Agamemnon called the girl to him, pretending she was to be married to Achilles. But this was just a trick – she was sacrificed on an altar. After the sacrifice the wind blew strong and the fleet set sail to Troy.

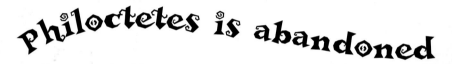

Philoctetes is abandoned

On the way to Troy the Greeks landed at the island of Tenedos. There, the archer Philoctetes was bitten on the foot by a snake. He was in agony and his wound was so bad that the Greeks left him there against his will and sailed away without him.

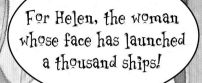

For Helen, the woman whose face has launched a thousand ships!

Ask the storyteller

Why did the Greeks want Achilles to fight with them?

Everyone knew that Achilles was the strongest hero of all, so it was vital that he joined the army. As a baby his mother had dipped him in the waters of the River Styx to make him invulnerable – so no harm could come to him. However, his heel had not touched the water and this was his weak point.

The Siege of Troy

When the army came ashore, the citizens and soldiers of Troy looked down on the Greeks from the strong walls the gods had helped build. Agamemnon and his men made camp outside the city and a siege began, which would last for ten long years.

In the tenth year, Agamemnon captured a girl called Chryseis and would not release her. Unfortunately, her father was one of Apollo's priests. This angered the god. He sent a plague upon the Greek army, which made them fear for their lives.

Achilles called a meeting and it was decreed that Agamemnon should return Chryseis. Agamemnon did this, but, to make up for his loss, stole Achilles's favourite slave-girl, Briseis. This caused a great argument between the two men. In anger, Achilles refused to have anything else to do with the fight against the Trojans. This was a terrible blow for Agamemnon, since he remembered Calchas's prophecy that Troy could not be conquered without Achilles.

How Odysseus escaped death

There was a prophecy which said that the first Greek who set foot on Trojan soil would be the first to die in battle. Knowing this, Odysseus, who was first to leave the ships, threw his shield to the ground and stood on it. Next out was Protesilaus. He followed Odysseus but was the first to tread on the land. The prophecy was fulfilled and he was the first to be killed.

Ask the storyteller

Did the Greeks give peace a chance?

Even after the conflict had started, the Greeks sent ambassadors who asked for Helen and the stolen treasure to be returned. But the Trojans would not listen. Instead, they threw insults and rubbish down on the Greeks from the safety of the city walls.

Let battle commence!

Even though the plague had claimed the lives of many of the Greeks, and Achilles was no longer fighting alongside him, Agamemnon chose to fight on. It was a bad choice to make. Unknown to him, Achilles, who was sulking, had called on the gods to punish Agamemnon – and all because he had freed Briseis, his slave-girl. The gods answered Achilles's call for help, and for a time they let the Trojans defeat the Greeks in one struggle after another. It looked as though the Trojans would win the war and send the Greeks back across the sea empty-handed. Many things happened in the tenth year of the Trojan War...

A lucky escape!

A truce was called, so that Paris and Menelaus could fight a duel. The winner would take Helen and the war would end. However, when Menelaus was about to kill Paris, the goddess Aphrodite, who was on Paris's side, made him vanish.

Athena interferes

The goddess Athena did not want the war to stop. She disguised herself as a Trojan and persuaded an archer to fire an arrow from the walls of Troy. His arrow struck Menelaus and wounded him. Firing an arrow broke the truce, and so the war started again.

Assassination!

The heroes Odysseus and Diomedes killed Rhesus, King of the Thracians, who was fighting on the side of the Trojans. They stole his pure white horses, which shone as bright as sunbeams, were as fast as the wind and could become invisible.

Thersites the coward

Thersites, the ugliest of the Greeks, demanded that Agamemnon abandon the war so that the men could return home safely to Greece. No one took any notice of Thersites. Odysseus beat him with his staff until he apologised for speaking out.

An even fight

Ajax, a mighty Greek, fought a duel with Hector, the bravest of the Trojans. The fight lasted all day, with neither man winning. When night fell, they exchanged gifts, and parted as equals.

Ask the storyteller

Where was Achilles while all this was happening?

Because of his argument with Agamemnon, Achilles, the bravest of all the Greeks, did not take part in the fighting. Instead, he stayed inside his tent with his friend Patroclus.

The fleet in flames

With help from the gods, Hector broke through the Greeks' defences on the beach and set their ships on fire. For as long as Achilles stayed out of the fighting, the gods helped the Trojans beat the Greeks.

Achilles kills Hector

With the war going against them, the Greeks feared the gods had deserted them – which they had! Their only hope of victory rested with Achilles. Agamemnon called on the hero to return to the war, promising to give Briseis back. He offered him treasure. He promised him 20 of the most beautiful women of Troy. He even offered the hand of one of his own daughters in marriage. But Achilles, still sulking, refused all Agamemnon's gifts.

When Hector the Trojan burned the Greeks' ships, Achilles's friend Patroclus begged to return to the fight. Achilles lent his own armour to Patroclus, to fool the Trojans into thinking it was actually Achilles who was fighting. But Hector was far stronger than Patroclus and soon killed him. Overcome with grief at the death of his friend, Achilles told Agamemnon their quarrel was over and that he would return to the war.

Achilles pursued Hector around the walls of Troy. Finally they fought and Achilles killed his enemy with a spear through his throat. He tied Hector's lifeless body to his chariot and dragged it around Troy, so the Trojans would see that their greatest warrior was dead.

The death of patroclus

After Hector had killed Patroclus, he stripped Achilles's armour from his dead body and wore it as his own. Achilles grieved for Patroclus and arranged a grand funeral for him, at which 12 Trojan prisoners were sacrificed to the gods. When Achilles killed Hector, he took his armour back.

The death of Achilles

Now that Achilles was back fighting, the war at last turned in favour of the Greeks. They began to defeat their Trojan enemy. Penthesilea, queen of the Amazons, came to fight with the Trojans. Although she fought bravely, Penthesilia was no match for Achilles and he cut her down. On seeing Achilles's admiration for the dead queen, Thersites mocked him. It was to be the final act of this ugly wretch. Achilles turned on Thersites and killed him, too.

But even Achilles's days were numbered. Although everyone believed he couldn't be harmed, he did have a weak spot. When Achilles and Paris met in combat, Apollo guided the Trojan's arrow towards the one part of Achilles's body left unprotected by the waters of the River Styx. The arrow struck Achilles in the heel and his life drained away. The hero of the Greeks was dead. Mighty Ajax carried Achilles's body to the Greeks' camp, where he was mourned for 17 days. His body was then burned on a funeral pyre and his ashes mixed with those of his friend, Patroclus.

Paris is killed

Philoctetes, abandoned on the island of Tenedos, was keeper of the bow and arrows of Heracles. He entered the war when Odysseus stole his weapons. He followed Odysseus, who led him to Troy. With a poisoned arrow, shot from the bow of Heracles, Philoctetes killed Paris.

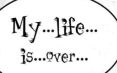

My...life... is...over...

Ask the storyteller

What happened to Ajax?

A contest was held to see who should be given Achilles's armour. Ajax expected to win, but he lost out to Odysseus. In a moment of despair and madness, he killed the sheep which the Greeks kept for food. Afraid of being mocked, he put his sword in the ground, fell on it and killed himself.

The Wooden Horse of Troy

It so happened the Greeks had captured a Trojan prophet who could see into the future. He said the Greeks must do three things if they were to capture Troy: bring Philoctetes to fight with them (they did and he killed Paris); the son of Achilles must fight in the war (he did); a sacred statue must be stolen from the Trojans (it was). So much for the Trojan's prediction – the siege continued.

It was the goddess Athena who told the Greeks what to do. On her instructions they built a wooden horse which soldiers could hide inside. These words were written on the outside of the horse: "For their return home, the Greeks dedicate this as thanks to Athena". The horse was dragged to Troy, and left outside its gates. Then, the Greek army boarded its ships and sailed away, pretending they had abandoned the war. Only one man called Sinon stayed behind.

Next morning, the Trojans could not believe their luck – the Greeks had gone. Sinon, who had let them capture him, told them that the horse was a gift to Athena. He said that the horse was too big for the Trojans to take inside their city. This made the Trojans more eager to bring it within the walls of Troy and prove the Greeks wrong.

Twelve brave men

No one knows how many men were hidden inside the wooden horse. The story is so old that the number is long forgotten. Some say there were 23 or 30, others say 50, 100 or even 3,000. I believe there were just twelve.

Ask the storyteller

Was everyone fooled by the Greeks' trickery?

Although some Trojans were suspicious about the Greeks' 'gift', only one man spoke out. He was a priest called Laocoon. However, the goddess Athena sent two giant sea-serpents, which killed both Laocoon and his two sons. The people thought that this was punishment for refusing the gift.

Come on, Sinon, tell us the truth.

The horse will fit if you say so...

The fall of Troy

The only way the horse could be brought into Troy was by taking down part of the city wall (the part built by Aeacus). With this done, it was dragged through the gap. The Trojans finally celebrated because they thought victory was theirs.

Inside the wooden horse, the Greek soldiers stayed still and quiet. They waited until nightfall when the Trojans were asleep, then crept from their hiding place and opened the gates to the city. From high up on the walls of Troy, Helen – the woman over whom the war had been fought – lit a torch. Its flame was seen from far away by the Greek army. This was their signal that Troy was open to attack.

The Greeks destroyed the city, ransacked its temples and looted its treasures. Priam, the King of Troy, was killed. Hecabe, his wife, and Cassandra, his daughter, were taken prisoner. The baby son of Hector, the Trojan's fallen warrior, was thrown from the city walls and his wife became a captive of the victorious Greeks.

Why Helen helped the Greeks

Helen had lived in Troy for many years. She had become the wife of Paris, the Trojan who had tricked her into leaving Sparta. In all this time she had wished to return to Greece. Odysseus told her that if she betrayed the Trojans her wish would come true.

Ask the storyteller

What happened to Helen?

Let us not forget that the Trojan War started because the Trojans had taken Helen, the most beautiful woman in the world, away from Menelaus, her husband. But this story has a happy ending. With the fall of Troy, Helen was reunited with Menelaus.

The return of the heroes

After ten years of war the heroes hoped to be home in a few days, but this was not to be. The gods were angry with the Greeks. They had not wanted Troy – a city they had helped build – to be so completely destroyed. They regarded the destruction of its temples as an act of sacrilege.

So, in punishment, the gods sent a great storm to batter the returning Greek fleet. Many ships were sunk, leaving only a few to reach safety. One was Agamemnon's ship, which was protected by the goddess Hera. Though he returned to his palace, a surprise awaited him. While he had been away his wife, Clytemnestra, had fallen in love with another man. She no longer wanted Agamemnon, so she murdered him while he was bathing.

Athena's anger

The goddess Athena had supported the Greeks all through the war, but she was angry when they turned the city to rubble. She punished them with a storm.

26

Ask the storyteller

Did Helen and Menelaus live happily ever after?

After the storm it took seven long years for Menelaus and Helen to travel home. When they finally returned to Sparta, they had been away from the city for a total of seventeen years. They spent the rest of their lives there. When Menelaus was old, Zeus took him to the Elysian fields and Apollo made Helen into a goddess.

The end of the story?

And so we reach the end of our storyteller's tale. However, the end of one story is often the beginning of the next. From the ruins of Troy came forth a Trojan hero – a leader who had fought the Greeks. His name was Aeneas. He fled the city, carrying his lame father, Anchises, on his shoulders, and his young son, Ascanius, in his arms. He also took with him objects which were sacred to the gods of Troy.

Aeneas travelled far and wide looking for a place to found a new kingdom. He moved to Thrace, then to the island of Delos and then to Crete, but he was not destined to settle in any of these places. Nor was he to find any peace in Sicily, the island on which his father died. Only when he reached Italy did his fortune change. He came to the River Tiber and entered the region ruled by King Latinus. Aeneas married the king's daughter, Lavinia, and founded a city which he named Lavinium, in her honour. When his son, Ascanius, was a man, he too founded a city in Italy. Many years later, Romulus, a descendant of Aeneas, founded yet another city, called Rome – perhaps you have heard of it.

Aeneas, father of the Romans

It was predicted that one day Aeneas would eat the plate his food came on, and the place where that happened would be his new home. On the banks of the River Tiber, in Italy, Aeneas ate the thin loaf of bread he was using as a plate. It was there that he founded the city of Lavinium.

We must start again my son, far away from Troy.

Ask the storyteller

What happened to Troy?

With its royal family dead, its population killed or sold into slavery, the city of Troy was in ruins, never to be lived in again. All that is left is its distant memory, which is kept alive through stories like this one.

Glossary

Amazons A race of warrior women who lived in Asia.

Ambassador An official sent to talk to the leaders of a foreign country.

Duel A fight between two people.

Elysian fields The Greek version of heaven.

Immortal A being who cannot die, such as a god.

Invulnerable Someone who is impossible to harm.

Lame Unable to walk.

Mortal A being who will die one day, or who can be killed.

Oath A promise.

Oracle A place where one goes to hear a prophecy.

Omen A sign that points to future events.

Prophecy A tale of what will happen in the future.

Prophet Someone who tells a prophecy.

Pyre A platform on which corpses are burnt.

Ransom A payment for somebody's safe return.

River Styx A river in the Underworld.

Sacrilege A crime against the gods.

Shrine A special place to worship the gods.

Truce An agreement to stop fighting.

Who's who

Achilles (a-KILL-eez) The strongest Greek soldier at Troy.

Aeacus (ee-AR-kus) A mortal who helped the gods build the walls of Troy.

Aeneas (en-EE-as) A Trojan who became father of the Romans.

Agamemnon (ag-a-MEM-non) Leader of the Greek army.

Ajax (AGE-ax) A Greek hero with great strength.

Anchises (an-KY-seez) Father of Aeneas.

Aphrodite (aff-ro-DY-tee) Goddess of love.

Apollo (a-POLL-oh) God of medicine and music.

Artemis (ARE-tee-miss) Goddess of hunting.

Ascanius (as-KAN-ee-us) Son of Aeneas.

Athena (a-THEE-na) Goddess of war.

Briseis (briss-AY-iss) A slave girl who belonged to Achilles.

Calchas (KAL-kass) A fortune-teller.

Cassandra (kass-AN-dra) Daughter of Priam.

Chryseis (kriss-AY-iss) A slave girl who belonged to Agamemnon.

Clytemnestra (kly-tum-NESS-tra) Wife of Agamemnon.

Diomedes (dy-o-MEE-deez) A leader of the Greeks.

Eris (AIR-iss) Goddess of strife.

Hector (HEK-tuh) The strongest Trojan soldier.

Hecabe (HEK-a-bee) Wife of Priam and queen of Troy.

Helen (HELL-un) Wife of King Menelaus of Sparta.

Hera (HEE-ra) Wife of Zeus and queen of the gods.

Heracles (HEH-ra-kleez) A Greek hero with great strength.

Hesione (hess-EYE-on-ee) Daughter of Laomedon.

Iphigeneia (iff-e-gen-EE-a) Daughter of Agamemnon.

Laocoon (lay-CO-on) A priest in Troy.

Laomedon (lay-MEE-don) Father of Priam and Hesione.

Lavinia (lav-IN-ee-yaa) Wife of Aeneas.

Menelaus (me-ne-LAY-us) King of Sparta.

Odysseus (od-ISS-ee-us) A Greek hero.

Paris (PA-riss) Son of Priam.

Patroclus (pa-TROK-luss) Best friend of Achilles.

Penthesilea (pen-tess-ILL-ee-a) Queen of the Amazons.

Philoctetes (fill-ock-TEET-eez) Keeper of the bow and arrows of Heracles.

Podarces (po-DAR-keez) Original name of Priam.

Poseidon (poss-EYE-don) God of the sea.

Priam (PRY-am) King of Troy.

Protesilaus (proh-TESS-ill-ay-us) The first Greek to die in the Trojan War.

Rhesus (REE-suss) A Thracian king.

Sinon (SY-non) A Greek spy.

Thersites (THUR-sit-eez) An ugly Greek soldier.

Tyndareus (tin-dah-RAY-us) Father of Helen.

Zeus (ZYOOS) King of the gods.

Index